The Mountain of Miracles

The Mountain of Miracles

Created by Cleous G. Young

The Mountain of Miracles
Formerly the Prophetic Artist

www.cleousyoung.com

Illustrated by: Robert Schoolcraft
Edited by: Penny Chase

Published by:

ARPress
45 Dan Road Suite 15
Canton MA 02021
Hotline: 1(888) 821-0229
Fax: 1(508) 545-7580

Ordering Information:
Quantity sales. Special discounts are available on quantity purchases by corporations, associations, and others. For details, contact the publisher at the address above.

Printed in the United States of America.

ISBN-13: Softcover 979-8-89676-687-2
eBook 979-8-89676-688-9

Library of Congress Control Number: 2025924881

TABLE OF CONTENTS

CHAPTER 1

The Strangers

In a small village, just beyond the mountains, there dwelt a group of villagers. The people lived as a strong supporting family. Everybody knew each other, helped each other, and had fun with each other. This village was a place of brotherly love, yet nobody knew about it, apart from the tight-knit community of people who lived there.

One day, while searching for herbal medicine, an old man and his grandson happened to find this place among the bushes. It was the grandson who forced him to go beyond the regular route that they traveled daily. The two stood silently and observed the villagers as they went about their ways. Based on what they observed from the arrangement of the housing, the villagers seemed like a group of people who valued one another. Grandfather also had a warm feeling inside and he knew that something was good about the village and its people. It was not long before they decided to introduce themselves to the people of the village.

The villagers were startled by the sight of two strangers entering their village, but Grandfather and David had a harmless look. The Leader also had a warm feeling about the two. He and the rest of the villagers gathered around them with no form of weaponry just a hand stretched forward. Once the introduction was pleasantly made, the villagers did not hesitate to show these two strangers the warm meaning of brotherly love. The two strangers felt right at home. Grandfather carefully noticed that the village consisted of old, young, short and tall people. No matter how old or young they looked, they all had a zestful appearance along with a slender body tone. They were full of vibrant energy and this allowed them to move quickly and freely while they went about their ways. There was nothing slouchy about these villagers and it reflected in the warm feeling that Grandfather had sensed.

David, on the other hand, noticed two differences between the villagers and the people from below. The first difference was the way they dressed. Their clothing consisted of woven material wrapped around them and sandals made of wood, cloth and vine. The second difference was how calmly they spoke to each other.

Soon the crickets started chirping and the villagers' shadows started getting longer. The villagers knew darkness was near and it was time for them to finish up whatever they were doing. The strangers had to leave, but before they left, they had to make a promise to the villagers. They could visit anytime, but they could never speak about the land and its people. The man and his grandson agreed to the promise.

Every day, these two strangers would visit the village of brotherly love, until they were no longer strangers. They were now known as Grandfather and David, the family from below. One day, while visiting their second home, something happened as they sat and enjoyed a good conversation. Time, along with the chirping of the crickets, had slipped their minds. It was total darkness. Grandfather and David had no idea how to find their way down the mountain, because they had never traveled that late at night because of grandfather's poor vision. So, they had no other choice but to spend the night. They were given a shelter and nice soft beds to sleep in. The shelter and beds were made out of large strong vines for significant reasons.

CHAPTER 2

A Strange Dream

Early before dawn, David woke up and tiptoed across the room to wake his grandfather, but to his surprise, grandfather was already awake. He said, "Grandfather, I had a strange dream."
The grandfather replied, "What was it about?"

"One day while we were coming up the mountain, there was a faint glow of an image that erased the trail behind us."
Grandfather looked at him curiously, "A faint glow of an image?!"
"Yes!"
"Where did it come from?" asked Grandfather.
"It just appeared behind us," replied David.
"What did the image look like?"
"I couldn't tell. The glow was too bright."
"Did it have a face, or arms, or legs? Did it have a body?"
"It disappeared before I could catch a good glimpse of it."
"Where was I in the dream?"
"You were in front of me."
"Did I see the image?"
"No, you were picking the leaves from the tree."

Grandfather could not picture the image David was talking about, as he thought about different bright glowing images he had seen. David saw the look on his grandfather's face, and knew that Grandfather had no idea what he was talking about in this strange dream. He looked around the shelter and saw a pencil, and a clean piece of paper. He took them and drew the image the best way he knew how. His grandfather looked at the picture and guessed what it was. Before he voiced his opinion on what he thought the image was, he carefully said all the information that David gave him with a soft voice. "It was a faint glow of an image, it erased the trail behind us, and it disappeared before you could catch a good glimpse of it?" said Grandfather.

"Yes."
"Mmm, all I can say, it must be an angel sent from God," stated Grandfather.
"From God! My father told me that there was no God," replied David.

Grandfather was shocked that David was told such a thing! "The percentage is very, very tiny of the people in the world who don't have a God, even if they don't believe in the one you do. But there is a God and many people do strongly believe in that God. Some even use different names to identify this God. God is as real as it gets," stated Grandfather.

Grandfather knew that a part of it was his fault, because he had never taught David about God either, even though he had lived with him for quite some time. At times, he himself had felt a little discouraged, and that there was no God to begin with. This discouragement came after he observed that some of his prayers weren't answered the way he expected; especially the one that he prayed for guidance, protection, and a safe journey for his wife and daughter while they traveled. The small boat they traveled on drifted beyond their control. It was three of them who traveled but he was more concerned about his wife and daughter. Rumors had it that the boat had capsized within an area that was beyond the passengers' swimming abilities. Grandfather's vision was very poor that day and he begged the rest of them: his wife, his daughter, and the son-in-law, not to cancel the planned trip because of this. They agreed and made plans to bring back sweet memories of the trip. Unfortunately, those plans didn't come to reality.

At one point, he had blamed himself for the loss, but quickly realized that God didn't answer the prayer that he prayed for them. At that moment, he became discouraged about whether or not there was a God, as he quickly blamed God for taking the two people who meant the most to him. It was around that time that David came to live with him. Therefore, he didn't want to impress his own confusion on David's young mind. One thing that kept him going was the many stories he had read. Now, he realized that it was better to be late than never as he answered, "There is a God, son. There is a God," continued Grandfather.

"What is this God like grandfather?" asked David curiously. "God is mightier than anything you could think of. Mightier than the sword. Mightier than the pen. Mightier than any storm. Plus, God can be anything you desire..."

David said, "I want this God of yours to be a doctor."

His grandfather replied, "God can be a doctor."

David shouted, "No! No! No! I want God to... " And he became quiet.

Then his grandfather said, "You want God to what?"

David answered with a concerned voice, "I want God to heal you, so we can stop searching the mountain for medicine to make you well."

His grandfather then said, "One day, God will heal me completely."

Grandfather regained his belief, and encouragement in the many stories that he had read about the miracles that God had done in the life of others. He strongly believed that a miracle would happen to him one day. It was then that he truly understood the saying, "Belief kills and Belief cures!" Thus, he just had to be patient and keep his belief strong and steady. This came after he suddenly started to realize that he too could have been on that boat. Also, that his only grandson, whom he now loved dearly, came to live with him and not some mean strangers who lived amongst them.

"Where can I find this God so I can ask for a special healing for you?" asked David.

His grandfather replied, "God is everywhere!"

David exclaimed, "Everywhere? Where?!"

His grandfather smiled, knowing that this was the moment to start teaching David about God; a task he realized that David's parents had not taught him.

Grandfather replied, "God is always inside of you, and all you have to do is make a call within."

David became quiet for a moment, and then curiously asked, "Did you call within you so you can be healed?"

Grandfather answered, "Yes."

David then asked, "So, how come you are not healed? Did God not answer when you called within?"

His grandfather looked at him and said, "It takes time, son. It takes time."

"So, you are healing, Grandfather?"

Grandfather replied, "Yes." Grandfather then asked David, "When we search the mountain for medicine, do we always find it?"

"Yes," answered David.

So his grandfather continued, "That's a part of God healing me." His grandfather then asked him if there was anything else in the dream.

"No, that's it," replied David.

Grandfather explained to David what he thought the dream meant. As grandfather explained the dream, he saw the fascinated look on David's face. Grandfather wasted no time, since he saw this as the perfect opportunity to continue the task of teaching him small things about God. This was done immediately, and David's knowledge about God started to grow. Grandfather felt proud, not only of the drawing, but also of David for wanting to learn more about God.

CHAPTER 3

A New Family

As it became light outside, they prepared to go down the mountain, but first Grandfather had to go and see the Leader of the village. He needed to ask the Leader about the decision he wanted to make. Grandfather told the Leader about the dream, and his belief that he and David were destined to become part of the village. The Leader, a man of great knowledge and understanding, felt no discomfort in such a decision. Many times, he had observed how happy they were when they interacted with the villagers, and how reluctant they were to return to the bottom of the mountain.

In fact, he had thought about such a transition, but didn't want to force the two to commit to being members before they were ready. He was also a man of strong faith, and knew that nothing shall happen before the time it was destined to. Grandfather and David knew about the dream, but they did not know about the many prayers that the Leader had especially prayed for them. His heart was good and though he wanted them to become residents, he prayed that they found happiness, whether it was in the village or the town from below.

This strange dream of David's was confirmation that it was time for them to become residents of the village of brotherly love. Grandfather and David did not return to the mountain that day, because they had found medicine on their way down that morning. The medicine was made from the leaves of a plant that grew no taller than three feet. The leaves were boiled in fresh water and then drank while it was hot. On a daily basis, Grandfather would drink a cup or two depending on how he felt. He noticed that it really helped his conditions based on the days he drank it compared to when he didn't. The day that he had lost his family was the day that he ran out of medicine. Grandma had promised they would go in search of medicine as soon as she returned. That promise never came to reality either. This caused Grandfather and David to build a good and reliable bond between them, as David became the person who helped him search for healing medicine.

The next day they would return, but this time their welcome was made into a ceremony embracing them as the newest residents of the mountain. The Leader of the village had planned the ceremony, and he was the only one to hand them a gift at that moment. He specifically shared with Grandfather not to open the box until the ceremony was finished.

Grandfather accepted the gift with great appreciation. Although it was enclosed inside a sealed box, it sure gave Grandfather a warm feeling instantly as he became curious as to what was inside the box. The little ones of David's height brought him brotherly hugs, while the elders presented the same thing for Grandfather.

The joyful dancing of the villagers during the celebration, enticed David and his grandfather so much that they joined in. They laughed, they danced, they ate, they drank and the villagers were super delighted. They strongly believed that God was the provider of all the happiness, unity, and peace amongst the villagers. They were very happy, and so were Grandfather and David. They now belonged to the village, and their lives were about to change. No longer would they have to climb the mountain in search of medicine, or deal with the mean, selfish people from below. Grandfather felt strongly that they would not be missed, because they had never been asked about their daily trip to the mountain. Nobody even noticed when they left with a few belongings, even though this was unusual.

They had found joy and happiness, which was one of the answers to Grandfather's many prayers. The villagers strongly believed that happiness and medicine went hand in hand, for they had never seen a truly happy person who was ill. Therefore, they made Grandfather as happy as he could be. Although he did not know the name of the sickness, Grandfather surely felt that he was being healed. He no longer had to walk with a cane. He no longer coughed, and his vision started to get better immediately. He realized that David's strange dream had become a reality, for no longer would they need the trail. He also realized that he played a significant role in this healing process. His prayers for healing had landed him in a place where happiness was believed to be a natural healing medicine. As they danced amongst the villagers, joyful tears poured from Grandfather's eyes. He had finally felt the joy of his youth once again. A feeling he had not had in a very long time, which aligned perfectly with the proverb, 'laughter is good for the soul..."

For David, this would be his third home. He felt as if he were with his real parents before they had passed away. He wasn't aware of any other family members besides his grandfather, which forced his grandfather to become a parent once again. Now, seeing the tears of joy flow from his grandfather's eyes while he laughed, seeing him walk without his cane that he was so dependent on, made him realize that this God, must be real.

David was even more eager to learn about God. He realized that his seven years of traveling the mountain had ended and that God could answer his prayers in due time, if he prayed to God and believed, just as his Grandfather did. The place he had been visiting for the past three years, became his new home and provided him with a new family.

CHAPTER 4

The Gift of the Cross

As dark began to fall, it was time to end the ceremony. The melodious sound from the drums stopped. Grandfather saw that the drums were made out of tree barks. The barks were cut into rectangles and then set out to dry, alongside the branches that were used for the drumsticks. There were only five drums made available at a time and were only played by the five chosen children. Only five were chosen in order to let them who play become better at their daily practices. These five children were also responsible for the value that came from the drums and sticks; by making sure that they were in good standards at all times. To see value in it was the first step in knowing how to make it valuable for a long time. This was something important that Leader Shaheim taught them.

The villagers made a circle as though they were about to light a bonfire, and in the middle stood David and his grandfather. They waited patiently as the others prepared something special for them. Those who had prepared food and clothing gifts for them began to step forward. These gifts included jars of honey, strawberries, potatoes, corns, baskets of grapes, woven cloth for their clothing, cushiony blankets, sandals, and head gears. These gifts were freshly prepared, and the many that were given to David and Grandfather, made the belongings they had brought with them seem useless.

The Leader, seated in a chair made out of tree vines, asked Grandfather to bring forth the gift he had given him earlier. He did so and the Leader opened the box, also made of tree vines and leaves that carpeted and sealed the vines. Inside the box was a jade color cross made out of a rock that had a marble texture. It was said that this cross represented God's true love and the direct connection to God. It was also said that this cross could heal any sickness, but it should only be used on the members of the village, as it was specially handmade by one of the ancestors of the villagers.

Grandfather accepted the cross and as he held it, he was warmed by the heat the cross emitted. He hugged David tightly to show his appreciation. As tears of happiness fell from his eyes, he realized that David had been there for him all these years. He remembered the warm love and attention he got from David. The love and attention seemed as if they were the only sources of hope he had to stay alive when he was so sick. Although David was not sick, he wanted God to do a miracle for David as well, for he knew that David, his only grandson, had a pure heart.

Grandfather turned around, then kneeled before the Leader and said, "Leader Shaheim, I accept this gift with all my gratitude." Leader Shaheim replied with a booming voice, "Stand before me. I am not your King. There is no need for you to kneel before me, for we are all equal." He paused for a moment and continued, "You should only kneel when you pray to God, for it is a sign of humbleness."

He then hugged him and said, "Grandfather, I may be the Leader of the village, but there is no reason for you to treat me different from the others. We are all one, like the Yin and Yang. No one here is above anyone else, because we all balance each other out…"

Grandfather had gotten a clear understanding of what was expected of them. Shaheim was a great leader and he knew that superiority could bring fear to some people. Therefore, he allowed everyone to be superior in order to make them feel comfortable, but they must not forget the most important principle, respect. Whether one is young or old it should be given accordingly and received appropriately. This was the principle used to bring the villagers into one accord. It made the village a place that everyone loved, for they all respected and appreciated each other.

After the ceremony, Grandfather and David were shown to their shelter. It was made out of large vines and in it were a small table and two beds, which were also made of vines and large thick layers of blankets for comfort. It was said that everything that was significant, except the cross and the drums, were made from vines, for no other plant could grow or spread faster than the vine plant. They hoped their love could do the same for one another. These were the significant reasons why the things were made from the vine plant.

Each shelter in the village was exactly like the others, even Leader Shaheim's shelter. As they settled themselves and their belongings, Grandfather realized that it was the same shelter where they had slept when David had the strange dream. He saw the picture of the image that David had drawn and realized that it had life to it. It captured something worth staring at. He looked over at David, then at the picture, and knew that David had a special gift waiting to be revealed.

CHAPTER 5

The Baptism

The night passed quickly, and soon another day was creeping upon the village, but it was no regular day, at least for Grandfather and David. Their new lives had begun and the daily routine that they were used to was gone, as there was a new one to learn. The village on the mountain had ways that were known to every villager. Grandfather and David would have to be taught these ways, even though they had been visiting for the past three years. The ways of the village were only taught to the villagers and not strangers.

Mrs. Palmer, a lady of great wisdom, was a teacher in the village. She taught the children of the village about God and the works of God. She was also one of the adults that were responsible for guiding the children on a path from childhood to adulthood. She taught them such things as dancing, planting, harvesting, praying, and preparing a good meal. The children were formed into different groups to learn these things, but would come together as one union for meals and play. For instance, the group who did the harvesting would bring the harvest to another group, and that group would prepare the meal. This allowed all the villagers to enjoy the fruits of their labor.

Mrs. Palmer went to the shelter where Grandfather and David resided. They were greeted with a pleasant and specific membership handshake because they were no longer strangers to each other. Mrs. Palmer shared with them that they should come with her to the river, where their baptism would take place.

David asked, "Mrs. Palmer, what is a baptism?"

She replied, "A baptism is a ritual that is done to wash away your sins of the old life and redeem your new life. It's like having a dirty plate. You wash off the dirt with the water so it can be used once again. But this time it will be cleaned and ready to be used without any form of dirt. The key factor is the water: it washes away your sins just as it washes the dirt from a plate."

He then asked, "Will grandfather be baptized too?"

She smiled and answered, "Yes, it's a requirement for all village members."

David had no more questions, so they all left and walked to the river where they would meet some of the other members of the village. At the river, Grandfather noticed other villagers being baptized, even though they were members already.

He asked Mrs. Palmer, "How come they are being baptized and they are members?"

She replied, "It's just a practice baptism. They are just learning how to do it, for one day we may need a new person to do the baptism." She also shared with him that this would be one of their daily routines.

"The baptism?" asked Grandfather.

She replied calmly, "No, we all come here early to wash up and rejuvenate our body from our nightly rest. The villagers who come here the earliest are the ones who go back and prepare the first meal."

They all gathered around and waited for Grandfather to enter the water, for he would be the first of the two. In the middle of the circle was Tom the Baptist. He waited patiently as Grandfather slowly entered the water. Tom said a small prayer as Grandfather placed his right hand over his heart as he was instructed. After the prayer, Grandfather used the other hand and closed his nostrils. While Tom stood beside him, he secured Grandfather's right hand with a tighter grip. He slowly dunked him forward instead of backwards, as a symbol to move his life in a forward motion. In a few minutes the first baptism was completed. David started to make his way towards the water, when Tom the Baptist felt a strong anointing upon him. He knew that there was something special about David. Tom the Baptist felt the same way when he had baptized Shaheim before he became the Leader.

As Tom pulled David from below the water, he realized that the anointing of the Holy Spirit was upon David. The last baptism was completed and they all strolled back to the village in silence, as they honored the two whom they had baptized. Tom kept an eye on David, as they traveled from the riverbed to the center of the village.

CHAPTER 6

A Special Anointing

Back at the village, breakfast was ready. Everyone gathered where the ceremony had taken place in the center of the village. Every family engagement took place here, except the ritual of baptism. They spoke calmly and complemented the people who prepared the meal. Then, each person was served a full meal that could last until dusk, when the next meal would be served. They believed the first meal was the most important one and it should be well prepared. This allowed them to start their day off right with enough energy to maintain their body's energy until dusk. A prayer was said before and after the meal. Leader Shaheim knew that not every first meal would carry the members throughout the day, but he believed that a good prayer could help them get through their hunger.

David went with Mrs. Palmer's group, and Grandfather went with John, the leader of the planting group. Tom the Baptist hurried over to Mrs. Palmer and led her to the side while the group waited for her. He finally explained to her what had happened at the river earlier when he had felt that David was anointed. She replied, "Everyone on this mountain is anointed."

Tom the Baptist then said, "Yes! Indeed that is true, but I felt the same strength of the Spirit as I did when I baptized Leader Shaheim."

They both turned and looked at David and wondered what special anointing he had. As they stared at him curiously they noticed that the other groups were leaving. Mrs. Palmer hurried over and began to lead the children to the river, for it was said that the water represents the new life of God, and this was where she taught all her groups. Time went by, and it drew closer to midday. It was said that God did majestic works at mid-day; therefore, they reserved that moment in honor of God. They all headed towards the center of the village along with the other groups. No matter what was being done, everyone stopped and returned to the center of the village, for it was time to give thanks, praises and honor to God. This was another part of their daily routine.

They would form a circle, and in the middle of the circle was a pail of water with a vine in it. One person was chosen to pray, but it didn't matter who it was; everyone was anointed. The person who was chosen would pray over the water and then anoint each villager in the circle with the vine. Another person was chosen to offer a prayer of thanks, and everybody would hold hands and kneel with their eyes closed. After giving honor to God, some of the children and adults were given time to go back and finish what they were doing, while others got ready for the next part of their day.

Now, everything seemed familiar to Grandfather and David since this was the time of the day when they used to visit. The villagers who were chosen for the next activity would do something fun, such as teaching new songs, dancing, reading from the Scripture, or a drama reenacting the works of one of God's miracles. This would last until dusk when a different group from that of the morning would serve supper; the last activity of the day. The next day the routine would be the same, but would be done by another group.

They all went into their shelters before it got dark, for it was said that only evildoers walked about in the dark. As Grandfather and David rested in their shelter, they talked about their day.

Grandfather asked, "How was your day?"

David said, "Very good, and yours?"

He replied joyfully, "It was marvelous! It felt like the first time I did something I have always wanted to do, yet everything I did today, I have done before!"

David said, “I know I’m not different from who I was yesterday, but I feel a little bit different.”

Grandfather thought of the best thing that could have made David feel the way he did, “That’s the power of a true baptism,” he replied.

CHAPTER 7

The Anointing Revealed

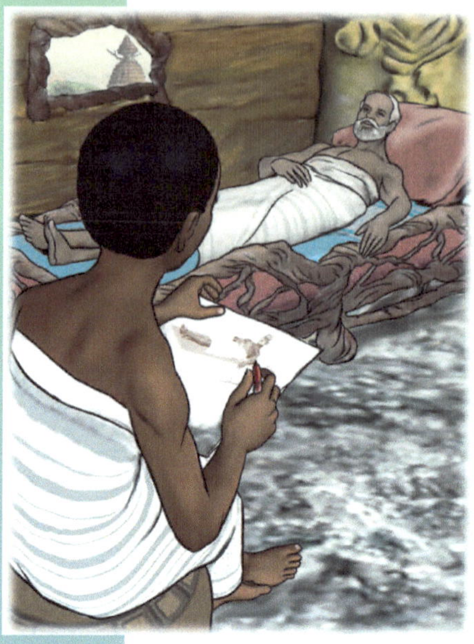

As they lay in their beds, there was silence in the room as their minds wandered. Unable to sleep, David gazed around the room and spotted the drawing he had made. He got up and put the lantern on the table closer to his bed along with getting the drawing and the pencil. He started to sketch the rest of his dream as he lay on his bed. Grandfather was unable to sleep as well. However, he kept his silence. He allowed David to work while he reminisced about David's first drawing and also about David feeling a little bit different, and tried to make sense out of the two. Soon both Grandfather and David were sound asleep. David fell asleep with his pencil still grasped in his hand and his drawing laid to the side of him.

Daylight crept up on the village, and the crowing of a rooster awakened Grandfather. He realized it was morning when he saw the sun's rays peeping through the creases of the shelter's vines, along with hearing the crowing of the rooster. It was a new day, and he noticed that his first day as a member of the village had passed. He also noticed that he had completed a full day without taking his medicine, and in his mind he said a small prayer, thanking God for this miracle.

Grandfather got up and walked across the room to wake David, so they could get ready to go to the river. He listened as some of the villagers passed their shelter. As David lay on the bed, Grandfather took the paper and looked at it. He noticed it was a full picture of the strange dream David had told him about. It was David, his grandfather, and the faint glow of an image erasing the path behind them.

It was drawn with such precision that if he hadn't seen what David was doing the night before, he would have thought a professional artist had drawn it and laid it there overnight. He woke up David and told him it was time to go to the river. As he was about to ask David about the drawing, he heard someone shouting his name. It was Tom the Baptist! He had stopped by to see if they were ready to go to the river. Tom the Baptist was also curious about what special anointing David had, and watched him closely throughout the day. The day consisted of the same activities, and the only difference was that David was in the harvest group and Grandfather was in the dancing group.

As it started getting dark, they all headed for their shelters, but not before some encouraging words were exchanged by all the villagers to end a good day. On their way to the shelter, Grandfather remembered the drawing and asked David about it. To his surprise, David had no recollection of what he was talking about. When they entered the shelter, Grandfather got the drawing and showed it to him. His memory of the drawing returned.

David said, "I remember when I saw the other drawing and I wanted to complete it, but I don't remember what happened after that..."

Grandfather thought for a moment, "You were probably so tired from the day that you fell asleep right after you finished. It seems as if God has anointed you with the talent to be an artist, for this is your second time drawing, and it looks as if you have been doing it for many, many years."

David then said with a soft voice, "Grandfather, I guess we both got a miracle from God."

Grandfather warmly replied, "Yes. I think we both did."

Grandfather held David's hands and whispered in a low voice a prayer thanking God. After the prayer Grandfather asked David to draw his picture. David took another clean sheet of paper, the pencil and started to draw his grandfather lying on his bed. When he was finished, he showed the picture to his grandfather. Again, Grandfather was amazed!

He looked at David and said, "Son, God has given you a special talent and you need to be very thankful, and promise me, promise me that you will use it as much as you can and as wisely as possible."

Grandfather had said these things to him, because he remembered the people from the town below. There were many who had lost what was given to them because they never used it or if they did, they did it unethically. He loved his only grandson and didn't want the same thing to happen to him.

"I will, Grandfather. I will," promised David.

CHAPTER 8

Divine Drawing, Called to Teach

David's future as an artist had just begun, because from that night on, he drew everything he saw, did, or was interested in. This went on for months. Every night David would do a drawing or two, depending on how he felt. The shelter started to look as if it were an art gallery. There were pictures of all sorts of things, such as the groups he was in, the things they did in the village, the town from below, the foods, the animals, and other groups he saw. He drew everything he laid eyes on or could imagine. These drawings were clear, precise and had life to them. The only living person who knew about these drawings was his grandfather.

Finally, David and Grandfather came to an agreement to show the rest of the villagers his drawings. It was David's turn to perform in the daily routine. He then went and got his drawings. As his drawings were displayed, they caught the eyes and attention of each villager, because they had never seen such works of art.

Tom the Baptist finally realized what anointing David had received as he recalled the day of the baptism. He gave Mrs. Palmer a special look across the circle to signal what he had previously shared with her. She nodded in return saying, yes, she agreed with him. From that day forward, David's drawings occupied every shelter in the village. From family portraits to even a small ant on a rock. He had rendered his service to every member of the village, and they respected and appreciated every single drawing he did.

His drawings became such an inspiration that other villagers started drawing, but none of their drawings could compete with David's drawings. The daily showings of their art became an activity that everybody enjoyed. The best part of it was that nobody would compete to see who the best was, for they already knew.

In fact, the other artists turned it into an art comedy, where they would draw to get a laugh instead of fame or fortune. As the months passed, the drawings were engraved in the hearts of the villagers. A thought came to one of the villager's mind and soon that thought started spreading to the minds of the other villagers. They decided to make an art group, and to ask David to be the teacher. He was given time to think about the offer. While David and his grandfather lay in their beds that night, he questioned Grandfather about it. He didn't know whether or not he should become a teacher.

He whispered, "Grandfather, I'm too young to become a teacher."

His grandfather laughed, "Son, God has given you this anointing, and God didn't think that you were too young. If you weren't too young to receive it, that means you are not too young to teach it, because learning has no age limit."

David quickly interrupted his grandfather before he could get the other words out, not understanding what he meant by, "learning has no age limit."

His grandfather then replied, "You never stop learning, no matter how old you are. You can still learn, even from a younger teacher. Furthermore, you are on the verge of adulthood."

Grandfather got up and walked over to David's bed. He then gently laid his right hand on David's shoulder and said, "You would also disappoint them if you didn't take the offer."

There was no question in David's mind; he woke up that morning fully decided. That same day, he went to Leader Shaheim and shared with him that he would be honored to be the teacher of the art group. Leader Shaheim was quite pleased with David's decision to take the offer. As a leader, he could see the talent in him not only to draw well, but also the ability to teach others to become better artists. That very day, an art group was formed, which consisted of both children and adults who were interested in becoming better artists. The art group did not change the daily routine of the villagers. It only enhanced it, because it was another learning experience for them to embark on, reinforcing the notion that "Learning has no age limit…"

CHAPTER 9

The Price of Greed

As the years went by, things began to change. After seeing the progress of the artwork among the villagers he taught, David made a solo decision without the consent of his grandfather. He decided that there would be a small price to pay for his teaching. His lessons would be exchanged for food, clothing and other items at a bargain price. This decision was quite a shock to the villagers, as they quickly brought it to the attention of Leader Shaheim. As the leader of the village of brotherly love, they expected him to find the best resolution for they had never before known greed from any villager.

Leader Shaheim had no idea what to do, for he and Grandfather had questioned David about his decision and came up with no answer. Leader Shaheim didn't want to dismiss him from the village out of fear that he would start spreading word about it. He also didn't want to cancel the art group, for it had captivated the hearts of the villagers.

The price of David's greed had led him to his own isolation, as he built his own shelter a short distance away from the rest of the shelters. He also became a disruption to the village's daily activities, for no longer did he attend them. He was like a single grain of cereal floating in a bowl of milk. He could drift anywhere he wanted. His lessons were no longer needed, because they had found a new teacher. The teacher was not as good as David but he taught the best way he knew how. Many of the adults found his teaching to be somewhat of a success, while many of the children wanted David back. Despite the unbalance of thoughts in the class, they realized that David had lost his teaching position because of greed. Therefore, they made sure the children were aware of the pivotal

principle that governed the village, respect. One by one the children slowly learned to respect the teacher accordingly and appreciated what he had to offer.

David's problems were just beginning, as he had broken his promise to his grandfather. His grandfather's sickness had returned and it seemed as if he had returned to the bottom of the mountain. He coughed like he once did, his sight became dull and luckily for him, he had not thrown away the cane that suddenly became part of his walking habit once again. David only visited him once a day and showed little compassion for him. His greed had fully blossomed and soon he was like a monster who had no pity for those around him. For he had everything he wanted and his drawings were still perfect. The villagers still pampered him and showed their brotherly love despite the greed they saw in him. They knew that God could change him and beneath that greedy monster was a child of God.

One day, a lady paid him a visit. She wanted him to do a drawing of her son by the river. She had chosen David because everyone went to him when they had something important to be drawn, and no one else could draw as well as him. The lady asked him if he could come to the river the next day and do a drawing of her son.

David replied immediately as soon as she finished her last word, "What shall the fee be?"

She answered, "My breakfast."

But that wasn't enough for this greedy monster who added, "Your son's breakfast too; take it or leave it!"

She paused for a while as she thought about it. It was her only son and she had no picture of him, so it influenced her decision; she spoke softly and said, “Okay.”

The next morning David went to the river. The son sat on a huge rock that the children would normally climb and leap off to make a big splash in the river. Everyone else was in the water, bathing, playing, and practicing baptism. As David took quick glances at the boy and slowly drew him, a strong gust of wind blew the child off the rock onto the hard ground. They all ran over to help the boy, except David who stood there without pity looking as the crowd surrounded the boy.

While they tended to the boy’s crying and suffering, David returned to his shelter and showed no compassion for the little boy’s injury. He would wait for another customer, which he knew would come, for no other teacher’s drawings could compare to his. The boy had fallen on his back on the hard ground and injured his spine. His legs were paralyzed and all the villagers were full of sorrow about the incident, except David who was nowhere to be found. The price of one man’s greed was paid by others, most tragically by an innocent boy left paralyzed.

CHAPTER 10

Grandfather's Moment of Loss

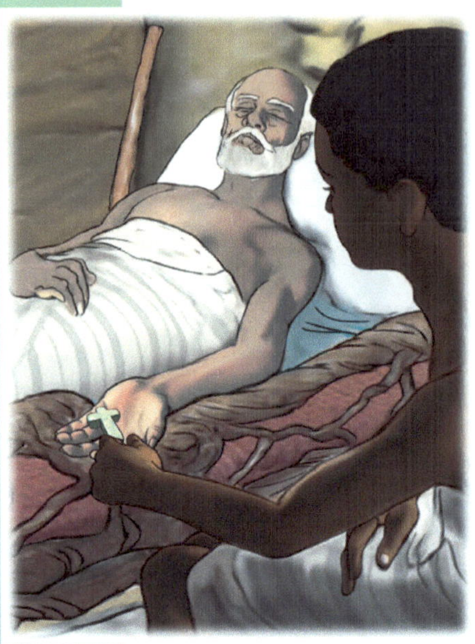

As the night drew near, a heavy knock on his door disturbed David from finishing up the drawing he started at the river. All he needed was a glimpse of the image and the drawing would be complete. It was Tom the Baptist. He came by to let David know that Grandfather's condition was worse, and that Grandfather wished to speak to him. They both hurried over to the shelter. David saw that all the villagers were there for the moral support of his grandfather. An emergency was the only exception that allowed for them to travel at night without being considered evildoers. This night was quite the emergency, as something evil was about to happen.

As he made his way to his grandfather's bed, he was just in time to see and hear something significant. His grandfather spoke with a shivering voice, "You have brought **evil** to the villagers, and you need to change, for these villagers still love you." He started coughing and David saw the pain in his grandfather's eyes, and asked about the cross.

They handed the cross to him and shared with him that it didn't work, because they had been trying it all night. David took the cross and immediately noticed how cold it felt. He laid the cross in the right hand of his grandfather, folded his fingers over it and started praying.

His grandfather whispered, "It is too…"

Grandfather never got to finish his last and final sentence, as he was sentenced to death because of David's broken promise. David showed slight sadness as he departed from the room in a rush. He had just lost his grandfather to death and soon he would be losing his customers, because they now believed that he was cursed. However, his biggest loss was still to come. When David went back to his shelter to continue his drawing, he realized that his drawing ability was dead as well. His frustration rose higher and higher, as he made loud, angry noises while he destroyed both interiors; of his own built shelter and of his own emotional well-being. The way he lived his life, a broken promise, an evildoer, a greedy monster, and showing no compassion for others, had brought these losses to him. These losses appeared when he least expected them, just like many of the diseases and illnesses we experienced in real life.

The villagers heard the noise and their minds began to wander. His insanity had left him breathless, as he lay on his bed with hard breathing and a disturbed mind! The shelter became as quiet as a lamb. They didn't hear any more noise or see any movement of his shadow; their minds began to wander even more. David's night had ended, for he was now fast asleep.

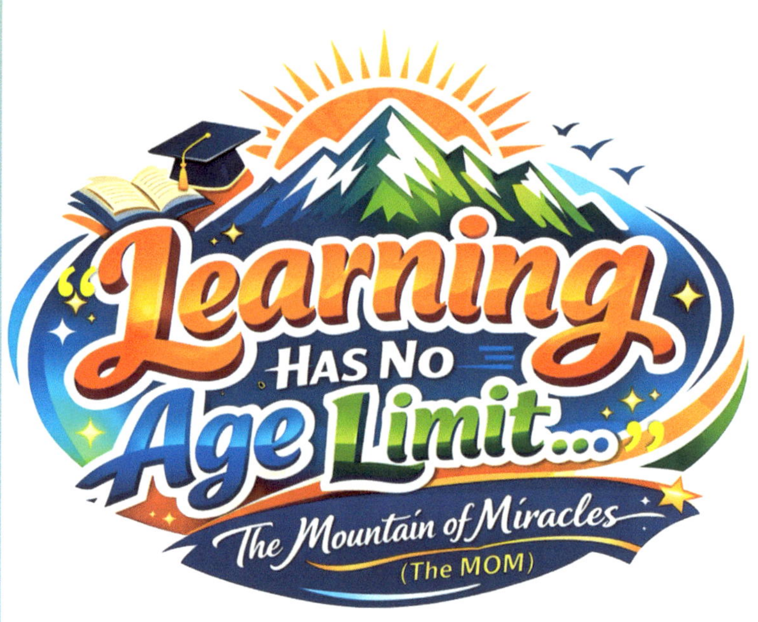
"Learning
HAS NO
Age Limit..."
The Mountain of Miracles
(The MOM)

CHAPTER 11

Lost, But Now Found

Days went by, but there was no sight of David. He didn't even attend the burial of his grandfather. When some of the villagers peeped from their shelters at night, they knew that he was still alive. They saw his shadow on several occasions as the rays from the lantern peeped through the vines. Nobody wanted to visit him for they believed that he was cursed because of his greed. They prayed for him and hoped that they could see the David they knew before he became the greedy monster.

The daily routine of the village continued despite these things. They strongly believed that prayers could change a person, yet one person should not change their traditional routine, especially a person who was once a visitor. They knew that he had enough food to last for a month or two, but they didn't know when they would see him again. They were a bit concerned about whether he would be alive or dead since they had not seen him.

Twenty-eight nights had passed by and they still didn't see him. Although they believed that he was cursed, they tried on numerous occasions to contact him. Their brotherly love for him was larger than what he had done. Time after time they tried knocking on his door or shouting his name, but none of their attempts were successful. David was defenseless, ashamed, and didn't answer even when he heard them calling his name. They even started to leave food at his door. When the food disappeared, they thought to themselves that he could still be alive. Although the food disappeared, they knew that wild animals could have been the ones who took it.

David, who had been alone for so long, balanced out whatever the villagers did. When they were asleep he would come out, and when they were awake, he would be sound-sound-sound asleep. David's quest in the dark would now classify him as an evildoer as the villagers believed. On the other hand, he didn't know what exactly was happening to him. Ever since he became a resident of the village he was always happy, because he had everything he wanted: plenty of food, more than enough clothing, his adopted families, but most of all, he was the best artist.

Then, suddenly, he had lost everything! He would practice night after night on his drawings and hoped that his anointing would return so he could face the villagers once again. But his drawings looked like those of a beginner and sometimes even worse, as if he had closed his eyes and drew them. He started to wonder if he could face the villagers. He now realized that he had taken advantage of them when he was strong.

The question he asked himself was, would they forgive him and accept him back into their fellowship so he could regain their brotherly love? The idea of changing surged in his mind night after night, for now he had nothing and was depressingly desperate for help. He was so desperate that at night he would go to the center of the village. There he would look for any leftovers that the other villagers had accidentally dropped while eating, which would make him compete with the wild animals for these leftovers. This way, he could at least have something to put in his stomach while he was up worrying at night.

He worried and worried and worried. The more desperate he became the more he worried. One night something changed about his thoughts. He began to worry less about whether the villagers would forgive him. Now, he remembered the teaching words of his grandfather and was more worried about whether God would forgive him. He began praying and even changed his schedule, so he could peep from his shelter to see what the villagers were doing. This overall change was happening in the background on his behalf even though he thought differently. By not having anything to eat and to put in his stomach, his body was in the state of fasting. Autophagy was taking place. Thus, what was bad for him, God was already working it out on his behalf. It goes to show that our worst state sometimes, isn't as bad as we are seeing it.

As he peeped through the cracks of the vine, sometimes he would join in with them while they did the entertainment, for he remembered the days when he used to be out there with them. He prayed and prayed for forgiveness, and then he would draw to see if God had forgiven him. However, his drawings remained the same. But he didn't give up praying, for he no longer wanted to be called the greedy monster or labeled as the evildoer who walked in the dark. He had found his own consciousness, as he dearly missed being with his grandfather. He regretted that his greed had caused him to lose both of his families; his grandfather and the villagers.

One thing that brought compassionate tears to his eyes, was when he peeped through the vines and saw the little boy who had fallen from the rock, being carried everywhere he needed to go. As he wiped the tears from his eyes with his clothing, he realized that greed was a hidden sickness he no longer wanted to carry. It had made him lonely and unhappy but most of all, it had made him lose the things that he had cherished the most. Now he fully understood this one parable of wisdom that his Grandfather had shared with him; "An ounce of prevention is worth more than one hundred pounds of cure."

David had lost many great things, but the desired change in his heart and in his thoughts caused him to find himself. This was something he never found even while his grandfather was alive or him being the best artist among the villagers. He knew his talent and anointing, but he never knew himself. Something his grandfather or parents never taught him. What he knew, returned, which were the old memories of the town from below. What he didn't know, which was himself, remained hidden. Now, he knew that he didn't want to be the greedy monster or be labeled the evildoer anymore. Now, he fully understood that there is an upright person inside of him. It was the combination of significant losses, an unknown autophagy, dedicated prayers, and his grandfather's stories that helped him reach this new level of self-consciousness of himself. Although it was a devastating overall loss, it became a true miracle to find this new level of self-consciousness. The greatest and highest life miracle of all...

CHAPTER 12

Anointed Once Again

One night, as David lay quietly in his bed, he heard a voice calling his name. He looked around and didn't see anyone. He heard the voice again and this time he looked up. He still didn't see anyone. The third time the voice called his name, he just answered without looking.

The voice continued and said, "My son, we have heard your prayers from the very first time, but we tested you to see if you had faith although there was no answer, and you passed. You were forgiven from your first sincere prayer and the villagers have also forgiven you."

David asked, "Where are you?"

And all he heard was the crowing of a rooster, which woke him up and to his surprise he had been dreaming. He quickly got up, reached for his pencil, a piece of clean paper, and began drawing. From the other shelters you could hear the echo of his voice when he shouted, "Yes!!!"

David had his anointed hands once again and he just kept on drawing, for he had a lot of catching up to do. He wanted to draw everything he had seen during the past few months, but was unable to. The villagers heard the shout and wondered what had happened. They were curious to see if he would come out, but their curiosity went on for days. David would draw from the time he woke up until he went back to sleep. This went on for days, until he had caught up with his drawings, except for one drawing.

One night, before he went to bed, he decided to draw what he had seen when he peeped from his shelter. He was drawing the villagers during their playtime, and when he was about to put his final touch on it, he noticed something strange in the drawing. He had seen someone among the entertainers. It was the little boy who fell from the rock. He tried very hard to picture the scene of that day, and remembered seeing the boy sitting beside his mother.

As David lay on his bed, observing the picture, he thought about what had happened. He started to think back to that time, years ago when he began drawing. He could not remember a single time he had observed something and had drawn it wrong. As a matter of fact, that's how he remembered doing most of his drawings. He would observe the things he wanted to draw and at night he would draw them. David took another look at the picture and noticed that the young boy's mother was sitting by herself with a space beside her. The space was large enough for another person to fit in it.

He thought about drawing the boy in the space beside her, but there would be twins in the drawing from the entertainers' routine. He also thought about erasing the boy from the entertainers, but that would mess up the drawing. So, he left it and went to sleep, but was amazed by what he drew.

Quietly, the villagers slept. You could hear the insects as they made their familiar sounds. With its bright light shining through the cracks of each shelter, the moon rested beautifully over the village of brotherly love. It was like the old days, peaceful and calm, and each star was visible, even to the smallest child. As David lay there asleep, another strange dream came upon him.

CHAPTER 13

Welcome Back

It was daylight, but David was sound-sound-sound asleep. Not even the crowing of the rooster could wake him. He had stayed up most of the night trying to figure out what he had drawn. It was majestic midday when he finally woke up, and was just in time to see the villagers getting ready for their next daily routine. He remembered the strange dream and decided that he would follow what the dream said.

The dream was that he should take the picture and show the mother of the boy. He peeped through the vines and watched them as they prayed. He prayed with them. Later, it was time for the daily entertainment. He took the drawing and took a deep breath as he opened the door. The villagers, although they were astonished to see him, ran over and gave him a big group hug. There were voices that shouted, “Thank you! God, thank you!” David felt as if he was a new member once again, as the blood in his heart warmed his whole body.

The villagers were very happy and so was David, for all of their prayers had been answered. Even the mother of the little boy who had fallen from the rock was rejoicing. They walked back to the center of the circle to continue their routine. Leader Shaheim gave his seat to David as he stood beside him and watched the entertainers. David was so happy that he almost forgot what he had come outside for. So, he interrupted the routine, but nobody objected because they all wanted to hear what he had to say.

David looked over at the little boy and his mother, and the boy sat right beside his mother and that’s how he remembered them. He told them about the last dream he had and as he told them, he showed them the picture. The villagers looked at the picture closely and saw the same thing David had seen. They also saw something that David had not paid attention to, which was the cross around the boy's neck. One of the villagers retrieved the cross and noticed that its warmth was restored. Leader Shaheim placed it around the boy's neck and prayed a special prayer for him. They continued with the entertainment till dusk, when the last meal was served. They all welcomed David back to the family. He accepted the welcome and wished his grandfather was there to physically witness it.

The night came quickly and the villagers headed towards their shelters. While David sat in his shelter, he decided to finish drawing the picture of the boy who fell from the rock. This was the one drawing he had not drawn. He wanted to save the most important one for last. When he was finished, he would give it to the mother in the morning, free of charge. The picture was drawn to perfection. He laid it to the side and then went straight to bed.

The next day he was awakened, not by the crowing of the rooster, but by the rays of the sun that shone brightly through the vines. While he was getting ready to go to the river with the other villagers, he heard a loud banging on his door. By the time he opened the door, someone had leapt on him and was hugging him tightly.

As he staggered backwards, he looked to see who it was, and realized that it was the little boy who fell from the rock. The mother stood outside with joyful tears streaming down the corners of her eyes. He invited her in and she also gave him a big hug. It was a passionate hug that was filled with gratitude, love and mostly forgiveness. The boy was walking just as he had drawn in his picture. The picture detailed the miracle but both knew that it came from the majestic works of God. The mother closed her eyes and whispered a prayer of thanks knowing that God had done a great miracle for her son.

Happiness was in the air as he got the picture, handed it to the mother, and redeemed himself. Now, he felt upright and was very conscious about himself. He knew deep down that he just did something worthy and noble. She gave him a kiss on his cheek to show her full appreciation. Silence captured the moment as words could not express the joy the three were feeling. When the three gathered their composure, they hurried down to the river to spread the miraculous news. He had lost someone who was dear to him and with due time he had gained a great miracle. In honor of his grandfather and his teachings, he returned to the original shelter. From that day forward, due to the miraculous gift from God, there was a Prophetic Artist who lived on top of the mountain. The same mountain that brought the villagers many miracles, and thus it was now known as The Mountain of Miracles.

To be continued…

The Parable of the Rising Tides:

The water that rises its tides, whether the ocean or the river, will flood the land with its powerful flow and cause the removal of any obstacles in its way. In the same way, when a person lifts their thoughts to greater heights—raising the tides of their mind to a mountainous level—every obstacle in their path is swept away. Old fears, doubts, and limitations are removed, making way for growth, clarity, and transformation. So, let your thoughts rise like the tides. Allow the powerful flow of your mind to clear away what holds you back, and you will find your life renewed and your path open for miracles.

Scripture:

Psalm 121: 1 "I will lift up mine eyes unto to the Hills, from whence cometh my help.

The Kitchen's Kettle Pouring Position

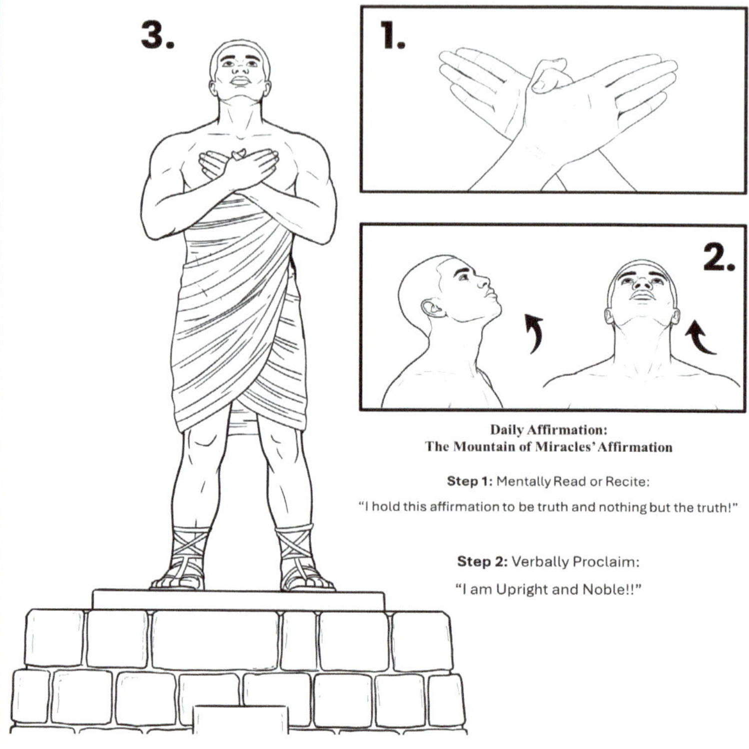

Affirmation's Process:

- Allow yourself to be in a calm and relaxed standing position.
- Follow the step in drawing number 1.
- Next, place your hands (Drawing #1) over your chest location.
- Mentally read or repeat the instruction of step 1 (3X)
- Then follow the step in drawing number 2.
- Finally, read aloud the instruction of step 2 (3X) in drawing number 3
- Afterwards, resume your normal everyday position. The End!
- Repeat daily and as necessary, especially before or during challenging decisions.

www.ingramcontent.com/pod-product-compliance
Ingram Content Group UK Ltd.
Pitfield, Milton Keynes, MK11 3LW, UK
UKHW060401300726
14090UKWH00001B/56

* 9 7 9 8 8 9 6 7 6 6 8 7 2 *